Ballet Academy

By Lorrie Mack

LONDON, NEW YORK,
MELBOURNE, MUNICH, AND DELHI

DK LONDON
Series Editor Deborah Lock
US Senior Editor Margaret Parrish
Project Art Editor Hoa Luc
Producers, preproduction
Francesca Wardell, Vikki Nousiainen

DK DELHI
Editor Nandini Gupta
Art Editor Jyotsna Julka
DTP Designer Anita Yadav
Picture Researcher Sakshi Saluja
Deputy Managing Editor Soma B. Chowdhury

Reading Consultant Linda Gambrell, Ph.D.
Subject Consultant Diane van Schoor,
Principal, Royal Ballet Lower School

First American Edition, 2014
Published in the United States by
DK Publishing
345 Hudson Street, 4th Floor
New York, New York 10014

14 15 16 17 18 10 9 8 7 6 5 4 3 2 1
001—256512—August/2014
Copyright © 2014 Dorling Kindersley Limited

Published in Great Britain by Dorling Kindersley Limited.

A catalog record for this book is available from the Library of Congress.

ISBN: 978-1-4654-1969-9 (paperback)
ISBN: 978-1-4654-1970-5 (hardcover)

DK books are available at special discounts when purchased in bulk for sales promotions, premiums, fund-raising,
or educational use. For details, contact: DK Publishing Special Markets, 345 Hudson Street, 4th Floor, New York,
New York 10014 or SpecialSales@dk.com.

Printed and bound in China by South China Printing Company.

The author and publisher would like to thank Nick Goddard
and Sarah-Jane Smith for their generous and valuable help.
The publisher would like to thank the following for their kind permission
to reproduce their photographs:
(Key: a-above; b-below/bottom; c-center; f-far; l-left; r-right; t-top)
20 Alamy Images: Florilegius. **21 Alamy Images:** Pictorial Press Ltd (bl). **The Bridgeman Art Library:** Richard
James Lane (1800-72) 1836 (colour litho), Chalon, Alfred-Edward (1780-1860) (after) / City of Westminster Archive
Centre, London, UK (tr). **25 Dreamstime.com:** Paula Ohreen (b). **30 Getty Images:** Rischgitz / Hulton Archive (bl).
31 Dorling Kindersley: Freed of London. **36 Alamy Images:** Archimage (cl). **Corbis:** Steve Raymer (br). **37 Alamy
Images:** Mark Cator / Imagestate Media Partners Limited - Impact Photos (b). **Getty Images:** David Cooper / Toronto
Star (tl). **38-39 Alamy Images:** Archimage. **39 Corbis:** Floris Leeuwenberg (tr). **43 Corbis:** Bettmann (bl); Selwyn
Tait / Sygma (cr). **44 Getty Images:** Imagno / Hulton Archive (cl). **45 Getty Images:** James Abbe / Hulton Archive (b);
Claude Harris / Hulton Archive (t). **47 Dreamstime.com:** Gregory Johnston (cr). **52-53 Getty Images:** Pablo Blazquez
Dominguez (b). **54 Corbis:** Yin Bogu / Xinhua Press (t); Robbie Jack (bl). **55 Corbis:** Robbie Jack (c); Stephanie Pilick /
epa (tr). **56-57 Corbis:** David Lees. **61 Corbis:** Marty Bicek / ZUMA Press (tr). **66 Dreamstime.com:** Lenanet (t).
68 Alamy Images: RIA Novosti (cr). **Getty Images:** Imagno / Hulton Archive (cl). **69 Getty Images:** Baron / Hulton
Archive (tl); Natalia Kolesnikova / AFP (cr). **70 Corbis:** Robbie Jack (cr, bl). **71 Corbis:** Robbie Jack (c, br); Belinsky
Yuri / ITAR-TASS Photo (tr). **72 Corbis:** Robbie Jack (cr, bl). **73 Corbis:** Robbie Jack (b). **Getty Images:**
The Washington Post (tr). **76 Dreamstime.com:** Gail Johnson. **78 Corbis:** Radius Images (b). **81 Getty Images:**
Lawrence Sawyer (c). **82 Getty Images:** mediaphotos / E+ (bl). **84 Getty Images:** Ian Gavan. **85 Corbis:** Robbie Jack
(t, cl); Maxim Shipenkov (cr). **91 Alamy Images:** ZUMA Press, Inc. (b). **92-93 Corbis:** Fabrizio Bensch / Reuters (b).
94 Dreamstime.com: Baiyi126 (t); Louella38 (b). **95 Dreamstime.com:** Louella38 (cb). **96 Corbis:** Leo Mason.
98 Corbis: Tadas Kazakevicius. **101 Corbis:** Robbie Jack. **102 Corbis:** Robbie Jack (cl); Kelly-Mooney Photography
(br). **102-103 Dreamstime.com:** Ana Sousa. **103 Corbis:** Robbie Jack (t, bl). **104 Corbis:** Robbie Jack (crb).
Getty Images: Gjon Mili / Time & Life Pictures. **105 Getty Images:** Paul Marotta (tl); John Phillips / UK Press (br).
115 Alamy Images: Archimage. **117 Corbis:** Nisian Hughes / Galeries. **118 Corbis:** Robbie Jack (cr).
119 Corbis: Robbie Jack. **120 Corbis:** Stephen Pond / EPA (br). **Getty Images:** Paul Hawthorne (cl).
121 Alamy Images: ITAR-TASS Photo Agency (t); RIA Novosti (br)

All other images © Dorling Kindersley
For further information see: www.dkimages.com

Discover more at
www.dk.com

Contents

Prologue

As soon as Lucy was born, music made her smile. When she learned to stand, she started bouncing up and down every time she heard a tune. Her parents took her to a toddlers' dance class, where the children skipped and jumped and pretended to be flowers. Lucy loved it, and she always cried when it was time to go home.

Later, she started ballet lessons. She watched the older children doing exercises at the barre, first on one side, then the other—it was all part of the magic and she couldn't wait to try. Soon she was going to classes twice a week, and then four times. She passed one exam, then another, and soon she knew she wanted to be a dancer.

Her teacher suggested she audition for a famous school in a far-away city—a special boarding school called a Ballet Academy, where pupils study regular subjects, but they learn to dance every day, too.

The first audition was being held near Lucy's town. If she was successful, she would be invited to the Academy itself for a final assessment. When the big day arrived, she was super nervous. The studio was huge, and there were many other candidates, but when the class started, she found the familiar movements and music reassuring. She did her very best, and before long, it was all over.

Just over a week later, a letter arrived with her results. She was too excited to open it herself, so her mom did.

"What does it say?" Lucy shouted. But she knew the answer from the beaming smile on her mother's face.

How It All Begins

Ballet dancers start training when they are very young—often under 10. They have to begin while their bodies are still growing so their bodies can be stretched and strengthened into special ballet shapes. Good teachers make sure this happens without any damage to young people's limbs.

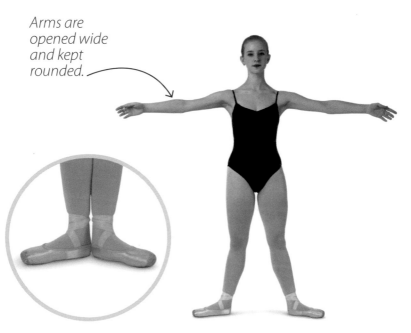

Arms are opened wide and kept rounded.

1st position

The feet are lined up so the heels touch and the toes point in opposite directions.

2nd position

The feet are in the same position as in 1st, but about the length of a foot apart.

One arm is curved in front.

One arm is curved around the face, slightly in front.

Arms form a soft oval with hands face-width apart.

3rd position

The feet are parallel with the heel of the front foot touching the middle of the back one.

4th position

Similar to 5th, except one foot is about its own length in front of the other.

5th position

The feet are fully crossed and together, so the toe of one touches the heel of the other.

Chapter 1
Chasing a Dream

Lucy put her bag down on the long wooden bench and opened the metal locker she had been assigned. Early that day, her parents had driven her to the Academy for her final assessment. She knew how special it was, because these teachers saw hundreds and hundreds of students from all over the country, and even the world, for their school. Now she was on the final short list and what she did today would affect the rest of her life. Would she go back to her own small ballet school, or would she become one of the handful of students who were chosen to live and study here?

Slowly, to calm her mind, she took from her bag all the things she needed for this important class: a simple leotard, a pair of socks, and her leather ballet slippers with the strip of elastic her mom had sewn across the instep. Then she dug down deep to find the combs, barrettes, and bobby pins a dancer needs to keep her hair neat and out of her face.

While she was getting ready, she noticed another student doing the same thing, and looking even more nervous than she felt.

"Hello," she said to the tall blonde girl. "I'm Lucy. Do you know anyone here?"

"No, and I wish I'd never come," the girl whispered, and Lucy could see her lip tremble a little. "What made me think I could get accepted here? I'm sure everyone's better than me."

Lucy smiled kindly. "I bet all the candidates feel the same—I do. But we would never have reached this far if the teachers hadn't seen something in us. So maybe we should both try to feel good about that. What's your name?"

"I'm Sarah. Thank you—I, er, I don't feel like I'm on my own anymore. Do you know anything about today?"

"Only that our class will be all girls," replied Lucy. "The boys have a separate audition." Each year, half the students chosen were boys and half were girls.

Lucy and Sarah began to chat about the class, and their practice clothes, and their favorite dancers, and soon they were both feeling brighter. Before long, a few other girls joined them in the locker room. There was a very pretty girl with a red braid, a slim tomboyish girl, and a tiny, very shy girl with huge dark eyes, who reminded Lucy of a mouse. Lucy found out that this girl's name was Joy, but they had no further time to talk. They were all being called for their class.

As always, the barre exercises calmed Lucy a little, so she could concentrate on all the important things: placing her body correctly, turning out her legs from the hips, arching her insteps, and still managing to stretch up as tall as she could through her whole body. When the barre work was over, the teacher gave the familiar instruction to "move into the center," so Lucy and the other girls formed neat rows, one behind the other, facing the big mirror.

Here they were asked to do more exercises, jumps, and a few step combinations—fast and slow—set by the teacher. These always made Lucy nervous, and, like most of the others, she made a few mistakes. She felt discouraged and slightly weary.

"Now, coming from the corner," instructed the voice.

Recognizing the signal for traveling steps diagonally across the room, the girls formed an orderly line.

Lucy waited to hear what the required step would be.

"Faille, assemblé," the teacher announced.

Whew! This wasn't the step she did best in the world, but it was one of the steps she loved most, with its swishing, leaping, and bounding across the floor.

When the Academy pianist started to play, Lucy squealed inside. The music he chose was from the Bluebird pas de deux in *Sleeping Beauty*—one of her very favorite pieces.

When her turn came, Lucy smiled and started off across the room. The music seemed to pulse right through her, lifting her precise steps off the ground, and she could never remember feeling happier. She wasn't frightened any longer; she was just dancing, and that was enough.

After that, the class finished, the girls made the traditional révérence (curtsey) to the teacher, and they straggled off, sweaty and out of breath, but relieved.

"What happens now?" wondered Sarah, as they headed for the shower. "Will someone come and get us?"

All the candidates knew they still had one more stage to go. Each one had to be examined by the Academy's physiotherapist and doctor. No matter how much talent budding dancers have, if their joints are too rigid, or too wobbly, if their feet aren't strong and flexible, if their backs don't arch, or if their legs can't turn out from the hips, they will be turned away. Also, if it looks as if any girls will grow too tall or any boys will develop the wrong proportions, their ballet careers will end before they begin.

At the end of the long day, when Lucy curled up in the back seat of her mom's car, she thought about how many things could go wrong. She knew what a hard life lay ahead if she was accepted to the Academy, and she knew how much disappointment and pain she would have to deal with if she became a dancer. But she never for one moment doubted that, here or somewhere else, she was going to do exactly that.

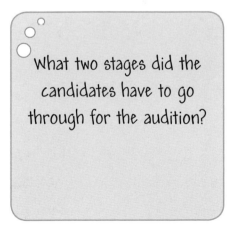

What two stages did the candidates have to go through for the audition?

Looking the Part

Ballet students wear practice clothes that are neat, easy to move in, washable, and close-fitting, so the teacher can see how each dancer stands and moves.

Leotards

Stretchy leotards are standard for girls: some have short sleeves, some have long sleeves, and some are sleeveless. Older girls wear tights, but short socks are common for younger students.

Jewelry

In ballet class, students are not usually allowed to wear jewelry, so nothing distracts from their line and movement. Also, flashy, scratchy, or dangly pieces, such as necklaces or bracelets, can catch or irritate.

Boys

Boys wear T-shirts and tights (usually footless) or shorts and socks, all made from soft, stretchy fabric.

Hair

Girls' hair is neat and tied back if it is long—straggly hair looks messy, and it can also fall in a dancer's eyes or fly around when she is turning.

Footwear

For class, dancers wear soft practice shoes (white, pink, or black) made from leather or fabric. They are anchored with stitched-on elastic across the instep. The drawstring around the top is pulled tight, tied, and then tucked in to give a snug fit.

The Birth of Ballet

Ballet is dancing to music in a very precise and formal way. Traditional ballets like *Swan Lake* and *Romeo and Juliet* tell a story, but many modern works just create a mood, or explore the link between music and movement.

Stepping back

Classical ballet developed from the court of Louis XIV, the king of France who reigned for 72 years from 1643 until 1715. In 1713, the first national ballet school was founded in Paris and grew into a company. There were no ballerinas because all the dancers were men! Ballet developed further in France, Italy, Scandinavia, and Russia.

17th century

Danish development

Inspired by the French, the Royal Danish Ballet was created as part of Copenhagen's Royal Theater when it opened in 1771. Its most important figure was Auguste Bournonville (born 1805), who became a great dancer and choreographer (creator) of hundreds of ballets. Some, like *La Sylphide* (shown), are still performed today.

18th century

Italian legends

During the early 19th century, the theater of La Scala in Milan was considered to be a leading center for Romantic ballet. Famous dancers that

trained at La Scala's excellent school included Carlotta Grisi and Pierina Legnani, who became a star in St. Petersburg, Russia.

19th century

Language of Dance

Because ballet was born in France, all its steps, positions, descriptions, and instructions are in French.

Changements *shon-j-MON* ("changings") are simple jumps from 5th or 3rd position in which the feet change place in the air, then land with the other foot in front.

Arabesque *ar-uh-BESK* (which means "in an Arabic shape") refers to a position where a dancer's weight is supported on one leg, and the other leg extends straight back.

En croix *on kwah* means "in the shape of a cross." At the barre, dancers work each leg in this shape—to the front, to the side, to the front, and to the side again.

Ballon *BAH-lon* ("ball-like") refers to the amount of spring or bounce in a dancer's movements.

Épaulement *ay-porl-MON* (épaule means "shoulder") refers to the graceful movement and placing of the head, neck, and shoulders.

Pirouette *peer-uh-WET* ("whirl around") describes spinning or turning on one leg, on pointe or demi-pointe.

Plié *plee-AY* ("to bend") indicates bending of one or both legs. A demi-plié is a half bend (shown). A grand plié is a full bend, where the body is lowered all the way down.

Pointe *pwant* refers to dancing on the toes. Demi-pointe ("half point") indicates the balls of the feet (shown), and en pointe means on tiptoes in pointe shoes.

Relevé *reh-leh-VAY* ("to rise") describes the way dancers elevate their body by lifting their heels off the floor.

Sauté *soh-TAY* means "jump" and jeté *she-TAY* means "throw." Jeté describes a jump from one foot to the other. A petit jeté is a small jump and a grande jeté is a big jump.

Chapter 2
Another World

In some ways, it seemed like a lifetime since Lucy had come to the Academy for her audition. The acceptance letter had arrived quickly, and the longed-for words jumped out: "We are pleased to offer you a place starting in September."

Now she was settling into her cozy dormitory, and she knew the time would come when the Academy's clattery stairs, snaking halls, echoing spaces, and quirky corners would become familiar. She was to share a room with three other new girls, and when she arrived on the first night, one of them already had her head buried in a locker, putting away her things. The figure turned around, and Lucy was delighted to see that it was Sarah, who had been her first friend when they had both felt so shaky at the audition. They shared a big hug, and then had a good look around their new quarters. In addition to beds and lockers, there were desks for homework and a shiny bathroom they all shared—a perfect little world. Just down the hall, there was a big common room with comfy chairs and sofas where they could relax or watch television.

Before long, Lucy realized she was hungry. "Let's go and find dinner," she suggested, nudging her roommate toward the door.

They had to ask directions twice, but eventually they found the enormous dining hall, with its endless counters arranged with meat and vegetables, cold dishes, hot dishes, and healthy, but scrumptious, desserts. They had never had the chance to choose their own meals before, so they both ended up with weird piles of pasta, sausages, salami, roast chicken, and chunks of homemade bread. They even managed to squeeze in dessert before they headed back

to the dorm, where they found their other roommates settling in. One of them Lucy had seen before—it was tiny Joy with the big eyes, who had also been at the audition class. The fourth girl looked familiar, too, but Lucy hadn't spoken to her yet. Her name was Jessie, and she had a wonderful giggle and the slimmest body Lucy had ever seen. Jessie was so delicate, she looked as though she could break.

By the time the girls had introduced themselves, exchanged information, and organized their own spaces, it was time to think about bed and look forward to the next morning—the first day of their life at the Academy. They were all very sleepy, and after a few cries of "night-night," the room was very quiet. Despite their uncomfortably full tummies, even Lucy and Sarah fell asleep quickly.

The next days passed by in an overwhelming blur. Each day began with a ballet class for the first-year students, with the girls all dressed identically in sleeveless leotards and pink ballet shoes. Later, everyone changed into neat shirts, blazers, skirts, and pants for academic classes, and then sometimes back into practice clothes or tracksuits for gymnastics. They ate all their meals in the dining room and soon learned to choose what to eat carefully.

Most exciting of all, Lucy and the other girls were fitted for their first pointe shoes!

They couldn't do much in them at first. They knew that feet have to be strengthened very slowly for pointe work. This meant repeating basic exercises like relevés and tendus over and over and over again.

None of the students realized how much pointe shoes hurt! Somehow, though, the pain didn't matter—just putting them on felt like a huge step forward.

"We have to suffer for our art," remarked Jessie, wincing and giggling at the same time. They were living their dreams.

Fairy Feet

Skimming across the stage on their toes, ballet dancers seem like magical creatures. To help create this effect, female dancers wear special shoes, called pointe shoes.

Where and when

Dancers wear pointe shoes for performances, rehearsals and special pointe classes. For ordinary class, all dancers wear soft shoes.

History

The first, lightly padded, pointe shoes were worn by ballerina Marie Taglioni in the 1830s.

Construction

Pointe shoes are put together inside out, using layers of fabric, paper, leather, and a rigid sole and shank—a thin strip added inside the sole for strength.

Grip

They are held on with satin ribbon, and often elastic across the instep—between the ball of the foot and the ankle. Sometimes, dancers glue the heels to their tights, too.

Adjustable

Dancers sew on their own ribbons so they can adjust the position and make the shoes secure.

Color

For most ballets, dancers wear pink tights so pointe shoes are pink, too, creating a graceful, unbroken line through the legs and feet.

Strength

Pointe shoes have stiffened (or "blocked") toes, but most of the necessary strength comes from the dancer's own feet and legs.

One afternoon toward the end of the first month, Lucy headed back to the dormitory to pick up a book and found Sarah curled up on her bed, sniffling. She rushed over and wrapped her arms around her friend.

"Sarah, what's wrong? Has something happened?" inquired Lucy, tenderly.

"Not really."

Lucy sat quietly and soon Sarah opened up. "It's fantastic here and I know how lucky I am, but everything feels so strange, and I really miss my mom and my cat, and even my horrible little brother."

Lucy had to smile, because she knew just what Sarah meant. She wasn't quite as miserable, but she was feeling lots of complicated things. She was excited and happy, but she felt nervous, too, and really, really lonely, in spite of all the new friends she had made. What she wanted were her old friends. She had never been away from home before and sometimes, late at night, she felt as if she would give anything in the world to be back there.

"I thought it was only me!" Lucy confessed. Soon, the girls were listing all the things and people, places and food they missed most, and in a funny way, that made them feel better and worse at the same time.

Lucy had an idea. "I know, nice Mrs. Matthews is usually in her office now. Let's go and talk to her."

When they started at the Academy, they were all assigned a teacher they could go to with any problems. Lucy had taken note of this, but she didn't pay much attention, since she couldn't imagine having problems here. Now she realized that being homesick was a very big problem indeed.

The two girls made their way to the staff offices and tapped softly on Mrs. Matthews' door.

"Come in." The teacher's voice was gentle.

Feeling a bit sheepish, they turned the handle and stepped inside. They hadn't really decided what they wanted to say, but in the end, they didn't have to say anything.

"Hello. It's Lucy and Sarah, isn't it? Is everything okay?" asked Mrs. Matthews, who was warm and friendly.

"Oh, we love it here," Lucy offered, her cheeks smudged with tears, "but…"

"But it's all a bit overwhelming, and you miss your mom?" Mrs. Matthews said, finishing the sentence. "I know," she continued. "Everyone does. It's okay to feel like that. I have an idea. Why don't we arrange for you both to go home one weekend soon?"

Suddenly, everything felt better. Somehow that simple idea hadn't occurred to Lucy and Sarah. They were so excited about their new world, but they had to be reminded that their old one was still there, too. They had learned something else that was really important—whenever they needed someone they could trust and talk to, Mrs. Matthews was there.

Academy Awards

Lots of ballet companies have their own school, but most are for older students. A few big companies also have boarding schools where younger boys and girls are given serious ballet training and academic teaching together.

White Lodge
(The Royal Ballet, Lower School, London, UK)

Vaganova Ballet Academy
(Maryinsky Ballet, St. Petersburg, Russia)

**National Ballet
School of Canada**
(Toronto, Canada)

Cuban National Ballet School
(Havana, Cuba)

Where the Work Gets Done

Come in and look around our dance studio. This is where we have classes every day to stay fit, flexible, and strong, and improve our technique. Some, often small, ballet schools provide music for class from an electric sound system, but we have real pianists who are used to playing for practice and rehearsal. They know just how to give us a lift when we're getting tired.

1. Floor

Dance-studio floors are always "sprung"—suspended slightly so they have enough bounce to absorb the impact of jumps. Studio floors are wooden, but some modern ones like ours have a vinyl (a kind of plastic) covering.

2. Mirrors

The huge mirrors allow us to examine every detail of our bodies, positions, and movements.

3. Barres

Around the walls, there are wall-mounted wooden barres that we use for support and stretching. We have two of them, mounted at different heights, but some studios have only one. Stored out of sight, there are extra, freestanding barres that can be set up in the middle of the floor, and then cleared away when they aren't needed.

Tucked in a corner of our studio is a small box of resin—a gritty powder that we rub into the soles of our shoes so we won't slip. Resin is a thick sap from evergreen trees that has been dried, hardened into lumps, and then crushed up ready for use.

3

BALLET ACADEMY TIMETABLE

	Monday	Tuesday
BREAKFAST 7:30 a.m.		
8:30 a.m.	Ballet: body conditioning	Ballet: body conditioning
9:00 a.m.	Ballet: classical	Ballet: classical
BREAK 10:30 a.m.		
11:00 a.m.	Math	French
11:40 a.m.	French	English
12:20 a.m.	History	English
LUNCH 1:00 p.m.		
2:00 p.m.	Drama	Computer science
2:40 p.m.	Science	Music
3:20 p.m.	Science	History
4:15 p.m.	Gymnastics	Country dancing
DINNER 5:15 p.m.		
PREP	History	Music
	Science	French

Wednesday	Thursday	Friday
Ballet: body conditioning	Ballet: body conditioning	Ballet: body conditioning
Ballet: classical	Ballet: classical	Ballet: classical
Geography	English	Math
Math	English	French
Music	Math	Computer science
Science	Geography	Music
Art	Religious studies	Technology
Art	Music	Technology
Ballet: character	Country dancing	Ballet: character
Art	English	Math
Geography	Religious studies	Technology

Chapter 3
New Horizons

As the months passed, there were countless fascinating new things for Lucy to learn. First, there were more kinds of dancing than she had ever dreamed about—not only dances from all over the world but modern and country styles, too. She kept up with all the ordinary subjects like math and science, but she enjoyed literature, art history, and music much more. Lucy even learned to play the violin! Most of all, she loved to learn about ballet: how it started, where the stories came from, and

all about the big stars like Anna Pavlova and Rudolf Nureyev. It wasn't particularly that she thought about any of this during ballet classes, but somehow the powerful tradition inspired everything she did.

Rudolf Nureyev in *Sleeping Beauty*

Anna Pavlova as *The Dying Swan*

The Divine Anna

The name of Anna Pavlova is familiar even to many people who don't know anything about ballet. Trained at the school of the Maryinsky Theater in St. Petersburg, Pavlova joined the Imperial Ballet Company there and became a prima ballerina in 1906. In 1913, she formed her own company.

Title of honor

The term "ballerina" doesn't refer to female ballet dancers in general, but it is reserved for a very high rank of principal dancer. An even greater title is prima (meaning "first") ballerina, and there are only ever one or two of these in any company.

Spreading the dance

Pavlova was not only a celebrated dancer and a glamorous celebrity, but also a pioneer who took her company all over the world, including the US, South America, Australia and New Zealand, China, Japan, India, and Africa. In some of the places she toured, people had never seen or heard of ballet.

The Dying Swan

Pavlova's most famous role, the Dying Swan, was created for her at the Imperial Ballet Company. Set to the music of "The Swan" from *Carnival of the Animals* by Camille Saint-Saens, it was only a few minutes long, but Pavlova's moving performance was incredibly popular with audiences. She performed this dance around 4,000 times during her career.

Autumn Leaves

Pavlova created a ballet called *Autumn Leaves* for her own company in 1918. With her as the star, it portrayed the opening of a chrysanthemum flower and its destruction by the wind.

Also, all the time Lucy was there, she worked incredibly hard. Like all dedicated dancers, she was constantly pushing her body. She wanted legs that not only reached her ears but also turned out and stayed there; jumps that hovered in the air; feet with incredibly high arches; and turns that went on and on. During her first year at the Academy, however, one more wish somehow found its way onto the list.

"Oh, Jessie, I want to be slim like you," she would say when the two girls stood together at the barre. Lucy's own body wasn't the least bit chubby, but she had gently rounded limbs and a curved belly. She hated them and longed for her friend's slender build.

"And I'd love to look like you!" would come the automatic reply from Jessie.

But once Lucy set her mind on

something, nothing got in her way. She started eating less and less at mealtimes so she would lose weight.

At first, she often felt hungry, but soon she noticed a difference in her body and the hunger went away. Lucy was thrilled. Soon, she stopped drinking milk, eating meat, and treating herself to anything sweet or creamy. A nice crisp apple and a tiny slice of cheese were sometimes all she wanted. She hardly noticed how tired she felt most of the time, or how much harder it was to extend her legs or support her balances.

One day, Mrs. Matthews asked to see her after dinner. Lucy felt incredibly nervous. What was wrong? Wasn't she improving fast enough? Had she failed her history test? Did she leave her locker in a mess? That day went very slowly, but at the first possible moment, she made her way to the familiar room.

"Hello. Come in and sit down."

Lucy felt better after seeing Mrs. Matthews' friendly face.

"Now my dear," said the teacher, coming straight to the point, "it looks to me as if you've lost some weight."

"Yes, I've tried really hard," replied Lucy, relieved and really pleased that her efforts had been noticed. But Mrs. Matthews didn't look pleased.

"And how have you been feeling?" the teacher asked.

"Well, I've been working extra hard, so I'm a bit tired, but fine really," responded Lucy. Her relief was fading and she couldn't quite figure out where this conversation was heading.

The voice was still kind, but it wasn't full of praise. "You always work hard, but we've noticed lately that your work hasn't been as strong or as sharp as it should be." Lucy was stunned. "And your body has lost some of its nice shape. Lucy, you're too thin. Tell me what you've been eating."

Lucy gave an account of her meager meals. A few moments ago, she had been  so proud of what she was doing, but as she described a daily diet of mostly carrot sticks, yogurt, and fruit, she began to suspect that it had all gone badly wrong.

With a more serious look than Lucy had seen before, Mrs. Matthews interrupted her. "The thing is, Lucy, your body is all you have to work with. How can it stay healthy if you don't give it enough food? Without protein, calcium, vitamins, and good fat, too, your muscles and bones can't grow correctly, and they'll never be flexible and strong enough for ballet. Think about it— if you don't feed plants, they wither and droop, and people do, too. At the moment, you're drooping a lot, aren't you?"

Lucy nodded, feeling foolish. She had never thought of these things.

"Now," said Mrs. Matthews, sounding reassuringly firm and practical, "I've arranged for you to see the nutritionist tomorrow. She'll help you choose the foods you should be eating and figure out the right amounts. Within a month, I would

like you to try and gain two or three pounds
and then we'll decide where to go from
there. How does that plan sound?"

"All right. Thank you, Mrs. Matthews."

Lucy slipped out of the room and headed
for her dormitory. She had made a big
mistake, and it suddenly hit her how much
damage she could have done. All the
students knew that at the Academy if your
technique wasn't up to standard or your
body wasn't working in the right way, you
would be asked to leave. You would be
treated kindly and taken care of and you
would be steered in the right direction, but
you would still be asked to leave.

The next night, the first-year students were due for one of their regular treats. It was the one they looked forward to most—a trip to the big Opera House to see the ballet company. The students were sometimes allowed to watch rehearsals, too, but there was something particularly enchanting about performances. The beautiful red-and-gold auditorium was glamorous but cozy at the same time. When the shimmering lights went down and the big velvet curtains swooshed up, everyone fell completely silent, knowing that whatever happened next would be extraordinary.

Tonight, the show was *Swan Lake*, and while the familiar overture set the scene in Lucy's mind, she had time to reflect on how much had happened in the past year. She had seen and learned many new things, and she was incredibly lucky to have a place in this very special world, but her foolishness had put her in danger of losing it all.

Highlights and Favorites

Everyone who loves ballet has a collection of special dances they look forward to seeing. Some well-known dances from the big classical ballets are particularly likely to feature on any list of favorites.

Baby swans, *Swan Lake*

In the flock of enchanted swans, there are four little swans, or cygnets, who perform a short but difficult dance together, holding hands, and performing the same movements at exactly the same time.

Bluebirds, *Sleeping Beauty*

When Sleeping Beauty finally marries her Prince, there is a huge wedding celebration. Among the guests who perform is a pair of fluttering bluebirds. This dance is often performed on its own as a concert piece.

Waltz of the Snowflakes, *The Nutcracker*

The "Waltz of the Snowflakes" is one of the most famous of all the enchanting tunes in *The Nutcracker*. During Clara's magical journey, she meets not only the beautiful dancing snowflakes but also dancing sweets.

Merry Widow, *La Fille Mal Gardée*

Lise, the heroine, is always trying to escape her worried mother, Widow Simone. With a group of Lise's friends, the Widow performs a delightful clog dance, which is based on real country dances of the past.

Setting the Scene

Stage sets for ballet pose more complicated problems than sets for plays. Of course, they have to create the right period and mood, but they must also leave plenty of room for dancers—sometimes lots of them—to move around. This is Nicholas Georgiadis's design for the ballroom scene in The Royal Ballet production of *Romeo and Juliet*.

The rich colors and the style of building suit the time in Italy when this drama is set.

1. Different levels make it possible for several parts of the action to happen at the same time, and still leave plenty of room for movement. The formal "Dance of the Knights" in this scene is one of the ballet's highlights.

2. The central stairs are adapted for several other main scenes in the ballet. They are part of the Verona town square in the outdoor set and they lead up the outside of Juliet's house to her balcony.

3. Multiple openings provide lots of places where dancers can get on and off stage easily. They also add to the drama by allowing Romeo to watch Juliet from the shadows, and his rival, Count Paris, to approach her without being seen.

Chapter 4
A Chance
to Dance

Before she knew it, Lucy wasn't a new girl anymore. She had swapped her short socks for the sleek pink tights that second-year students wore, and she felt as if she had always belonged at the Academy. At first, she had struggled a little with going home every few weeks, switching between one life and another. Now that routine felt completely natural.

At the same time, she and her friends were beginning to explore the world outside the school. They went out to visit art galleries and museums in a group, and they were being taken to see musicals, concerts, and plays as well as other dance companies. Best of all, Lucy discovered how important these things were. At first, she hadn't understood why looking at paintings, hearing orchestras play, or sitting through William Shakespeare's plays had anything to do with ballet. Now, however, she knew that once you care about dancing, the drama catches hold of you, too—and the music, the costumes, and the sets—and the more you learn about all these things, the more you feel part of what you do.

"Lucy, Lucy, have you seen the bulletin board?" whispered little Joy, as they passed in the corridor one day.

"I'm just heading that way. What's going on?"

"It's *The Nutcracker*," answered Joy. "The cast list is up and I'm in it!" Lucy wasn't sure if it was terror or delight she saw on Joy's face.

Nearly every December, the ballet company linked with the school would perform a season of *The Nutcracker* at the city's Opera House. This ballet full of Christmas magic includes some of the best-loved music in the world, so the performances would always sell out. But to the Academy students, *The Nutcracker* was special for another reason. It has lots of parts for children, so many of them get to appear on stage. Some are party guests, some are mice, some are toy soldiers, and some are clowns.

Lucy rushed to the bulletin board and ran her eye quickly down the list. She had two parts! She was a mouse in Act I and a clown in Act II. For a moment, she was disappointed and wished she could be a party guest and wear a fancy dress. When she thought about her parts, however, she realized how pleased she was with what she had. The mice were lots of fun, appearing in the middle of the night and attacking the toy soldiers around the Christmas tree. The clowns did more dance steps than any of the other children in the cast. That was the most extraordinary thing—she would actually be dancing on the Opera House stage!

Just before she turned away, she raised her glance to the top of the cast list. The ballerina role of the Sugar Plum Fairy was being shared between two principal dancers, and one of them was her absolute idol, Fiona Peters. When Lucy was a very little girl, her mom had taken her to see *Swan Lake* when the ballet company came to their city, and ever since, whenever she pictured a ballerina, it was Fiona as Odette. Once or twice, Lucy had seen her in rehearsal or in the Opera House cafeteria, but she was always too shy to get too close, or too embarrassed to watch her. Now she would be able to stare officially!

Plans for *The Nutcracker* went into action quickly. Early rehearsals were scheduled at the Academy so the students could learn their steps. To do this, they worked with two members of the ballet company who had performed lots of roles when they were young, and now taught them to the next generation of dancers. No actual cast members were there for the early run-throughs though, so Lucy and her friends had to leave spaces for the main characters while they went through all their movements.

Finally, it was time to travel to the Opera House to rehearse with the company and to visit the wardrobe department, where they would be fitted for their costumes. That first day, the mice went through the battle scene with the Nutcracker Prince and the Mouse King. When that rehearsal was over, everyone felt much less awkward, and, of course, the moves made so much more sense when everyone in the scene was involved.

Lucy wasn't nervous about the costume fitting, but she was intrigued about what would happen. She had to climb lots of stairs and explore several corridors before she found the wardrobe department, but as soon as she put her head around the door, she caught sight of Joy. Her little face shining, Joy was dressed as a party guest in an exquisite dress made of soft creamy lace that reached down to her ankles. It had long full sleeves and a pink satin sash that tied around her waist and fastened in a big bow at the back.

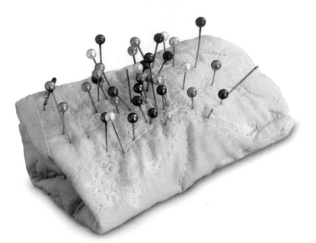

"Oh, Lucy, look!" she called out, and Lucy smiled and waved, relieved that her friend looked so happy.

One of the wardrobe assistants took Lucy away to fit her costumes. The mouse outfit wasn't as heavy as Lucy feared, but it was hot, and she knew the tail would take a while to get used to. The mice only ran around and waved swords though, so she was more worried about her clown costume. She tried it on, but didn't rush to the nearest mirror to check out the color (bright yellow with pink dots) or the style (close-fitting top and short, full skirt). Instead, Lucy headed for the nearest clear space and made sure she would be able to do all the steps she had worked so hard to learn.

"Just like a pro!" laughed the nice wardrobe girl, as she reached for her marking pins. Before the first night, she would alter both costumes to make sure they fit Lucy perfectly.

Why was Lucy more worried about her clown costume for *The Nutcracker?*

Tutu Timeline

Although female dancers wear many different styles of clothing, the tutu is the most closely associated with ballet. The first tutus were worn in the mid-1800s by Italian ballerina Marie Taglioni.

19th century

Romantic effect

Taglioni appeared in ballets such as *Giselle* and *La Sylphide* (shown), wearing dresses with long, flowing skirts. This style, called a Romantic or Taglioni tutu, is still worn in these ballets.

Showing more leg

By the end of the 1800s, tutus were shorter, to show off the dancers' legs and allow for freedom of movement. This is Italian ballerina Pierina Legnani in a production of *Swan Lake* in St. Petersburg, Russia.

20th century

21st century

Moving on

Through much of the 20th century, tutus were much shorter, but they still had a graduated, skirtlike shape. This is English ballerina Margot Fonteyn wearing her *Firebird* costume in the 1950s.

Tutus today

All these classic tutus are still used, but most modern ones are even shorter, sticking almost straight out from a slightly lowered waist. They are called French or pancake tutus. This is Bolshoi ballerina Svetlana Zakharova in her role as Aurora in *Sleeping Beauty*.

69

Captivating Creatures

Performing intricate and exhausting dances on stage is always hard, but sometimes artists have to cope with animal costumes and masks as well. These delightful, quirky characters appear in several famous ballets.

Squirrel Nutkin

Ballet: *The Tales of Beatrix Potter*
Role: mischievous squirrel who teases an owl

Puss in Boots and the White Cat

Ballet: *Sleeping Beauty*
Role: fairy-tale guests at Aurora's wedding

Bottom

Ballet: *The Dream*
(adapted from Shakespeare's
A Midsummer Night's Dream)
Role: country workman given
a donkey's head by the fairy Puck

Farmyard chickens

Ballet: *La Fille Mal Gardée*
Role: between-scenes
entertainment featuring
a rooster and four hens

Mouse King

Ballet: *The Nutcracker*
Role: warrior mouse who
leads marauding mice into
battle against a troop of toy
soldiers that defeats them

Full of Character

Some roles in story ballets are "character" parts. This means the dancers move around in a natural way rather than performing ballet steps and wear ordinary stage costumes.

DOUBLE TROUBLE

We are the Ugly Sisters in *Cinderella*. Our "characters" are often played by men in silly costumes and makeup. We wear our best finery to impress the prince! In all types of theater, parts where men dress up as women (or women dress up as men) are called "travesty" roles.

DOLL DOCTOR

I am the crusty old toymaker, Dr. Coppélius, in *Coppélia*. This ballet is named after the doll I made, who I believe I can bring to life. Franz, the boyfriend of a village girl Swanilda, thinks my Coppélia is a real girl and flirts with her. Swanilda sneaks into my workshop and pretends to be my precious doll, fooling us all.

DANCED TO DEATH

I am Hilarion, the village gamekeeper, in *Giselle*. My heart is broken when Giselle, a village maiden whom I adore, takes up with a wandering peasant. He is actually a nobleman and already engaged so she kills herself. In deep sorrow, I visit her grave but she has become one of the wilis—ghostly girls who dance men to death. I try pleading for my life, but the wilis will not listen.

GOOD FRIAR

I am Friar Laurence, a very important character in *Romeo and Juliet*. I not only marry the lovers, but also give them support and advice. It was with good intentions that I provided Juliet with the potion that leads to the story's tragic ending.

Chapter 5
A Dream in Peril

Over the next few weeks, Lucy didn't have much time to think. All the students still had to do ballet class every morning, including Saturdays, now that they were older. They also had to fit in all their gymnastic and training sessions, keep up with their regular subjects plus the homework, as well as shuttle back and forth to the Opera House for rehearsals.

As time went on, she began to enjoy the fairy-tale battle between the mice and the toy soldiers and feel more confident

about the clown dance, which was much more technical. Sarah was a clown, too, which helped a lot, and Jessie was at the clown rehearsals, even though she didn't have a part. Jessie was an understudy, which meant that she and another girl learned the dance anyway, so if any of the first cast couldn't perform, they could step in.

This year, *The Nutcracker* felt even more important than Christmas itself, and the students hadn't been able to give any thought to buying presents. So a group of them decided to arrange a visit to the nearest town. Following Academy rules, they had to be supervised and Mrs. Matthews agreed to go with them. They also had to wear their uniforms.

Wrapped up warm against the wintry cold, they were enchanted to be walking through the pretty streets with snowflakes coming down, Christmas carols floating out of every store, and windows adorned with festive displays. It took Lucy a long time to decide what to buy, but she was happy with her choices—a silky scarf for her mom, a book about golf for her dad, and a big bottle of delicious-smelling body lotion for Sarah.

All too soon, it was time to go back to the Academy, but the afternoon had been so special that Lucy wanted to hold a picture of it in her mind. She was taking one last look around, when she heard the big clock in the square start to chime. Without thinking, she looked up just as she stepped on a nasty patch of ice. She felt herself fall, and time seemed to move incredibly slowly. She felt embarrassed, but there was nothing she could do to stop her slide.

"Aaaaaaaaaaah!" she cried, as Sarah and Mrs. Matthews tried to catch hold of her, but it was too late. Lucy went down hard onto the solid pavement. Her foot folded under her and a sharp pain shot through her ankle.

"Are you all right?" everyone asked at once. Lucy desperately wanted to say "yes," but the pain told her that something was very wrong.

The other girls helped her up and found a nearby bench where she could sit. Lucy tried very hard to be brave, but she felt really shaky and she couldn't stop the tears from pouring down her face. Partly, she was in shock, but mostly, she had begun to panic about *The Nutcracker*.

"Okay," said Mrs. Matthews, "let's find a taxi and get you back to the Academy."

By the time they arrived, Lucy's ankle was throbbing, and when she pulled her boots off, she could see that it was badly swollen. Luckily, Dr. Nicholas, the regular school doctor, was there that afternoon. He examined her carefully and tried to reassure her, but he was clearly worried and didn't intend to take any chances.

"I don't think it's broken," the doctor declared. "It's probably a sprain, but let's get you to hospital for an X-ray, just to be sure." The word "broken" went straight through Lucy's heart.

The next couple of hours were a blur. A taxi came and took Lucy and Mrs. Matthews to the local emergency room. Fortunately, it wasn't busy and they didn't have to wait too long. A doctor examined her and asked what had happened, and Mrs. Matthews explained. He smiled and said the same thing as

Dr. Nicholas. "It looks like a sprain, but I will arrange for an X-ray."

Shortly afterward, Lucy was in a wheelchair and a humming orderly was whisking her off to a big room, where a technician took several pictures of her ankle.

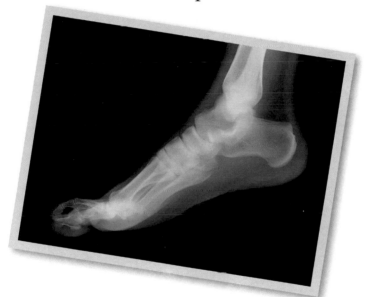

The pictures were ready quickly and the news was good. Lucy's ankle wasn't broken, but she would have to keep off it for a couple of weeks.

Soon she was back at the Academy with Dr. Nicholas, who understood dancers' injuries and knew exactly how much strain they put on their bodies.

"Will I be able to make *The Nutcracker*?" Lucy asked as soon as he sat down.

"I'm sorry, Lucy, I don't know. I'm going to tape your ankle and the nurse will do that again every day. For now, I want you to rest, keep your leg elevated, and put ice on it regularly to get the swelling down. All we can do is wait."

Lucy thought she would burst with frustration. She had imagined that by now she would at least know how things stood. At the moment, all she could do was make sure she followed Dr. Nicholas's advice exactly, and hope.

At first, she rested all the time, but after a few days, he gave her permission to move around a bit and try a few stretches. However limiting this was, at least it meant that she could attend rehearsals with the others so she wouldn't forget her steps.

As it turned out, watching rehearsals proved incredibly hard, too. Jessie was dancing Lucy's clown part and she was very good. The old insecurities came back about how lovely and slim Jessie was, and Lucy couldn't stop herself from worrying. But all the worrying in the world wouldn't help, and for the moment, she had to face the hardest task in the world for her—doing almost nothing.

Fairies, Magicians, and Spirits

Many ballets, especially the well-known classics, involve some kind of magic. Fairies, magicians, ghosts, sorcerers, and witches have wide-ranging powers over the main characters. Some use these powers for good, but many are pure evil.

Enchanted maidens

In *Swan Lake*, all the swans plus their queen, Odette, were young maidens before Rothbart the evil magician turned them into birds. They can only become human again if a man swears his love for Odette.

Graceful ghosts

In some ballets, the lead character and the corps de ballet are all supernatural beings: the swans, including the Swan Queen, in *Swan Lake* are enchanted maidens; the title characters in both *La Sylphide* and *Les Sylphides* are invisible creatures of the air; and all the wilis in *Giselle* (shown) are the ghosts of young girls.

Magic gift

During the Christmas party at the beginning of *The Nutcracker*, Herr Drosselmeyer arrives. He is not only a magician but also Clara's godfather, and he brings her a very special present—a nutcracker doll.

Bad fairy

Only good fairies are invited to the christening of Princess Aurora in *Sleeping Beauty*. The evil fairy Carabosse, angry and insulted that she was left out, curses the baby, promising that one day she will prick her finger and die. When that day arrives, Carabosse is there.

Making Signs

In the past, ballets were popular entertainments like movies and rock concerts. Often, parts of the story were told in a special language called "mime"— a collection of gestures that expresses words and ideas. Early audiences would have been familiar with these gestures, so they could follow the plots easily. Why not try some?

▷ See
Position your pointed index fingers just below your eyes, then move them down and away from your face.

▷ Come
Lift both of your arms in the same direction and round them gently in a graceful inviting arc, keeping your elbows down and your hands turned up. Then lower both of your arms and bring them close to your body.

▷ Dance
Raise softly curved arms over your head, then circle your hands around each other smoothly and widely.

▷ No

With palms facing down, cross your hands at the wrists, open them, and then cross again. Finally, open firmly as if brushing aside all argument.

◁ Sleep

Tilt your head and form a pillow with your arms.

▷ Die

Open your arms and form your hands into tight fists. Then cross your forearms in front of you and drop them with a swift, forceful movement.

▷ Marry

Extend both hands in front of your body and point to the base of your left ring finger with the index finger of your right hand.

Chapter 6
In the
Limelight

In just under a week, five-and-a-half-days—Lucy was counting—the nurse advised her to start physiotherapy. Russell, the Academy physiotherapist, was a familiar and reassuring figure to all the students, so Lucy couldn't wait for him to get started.

At their first session, Russell explained that sprains are injuries to ligaments—tough tissues that hold bones together to make joints stable. With a bad sprain, these tissues get torn and healing takes a long time. However, even though Lucy's ankle had hurt really badly when she fell, her ligaments weren't torn, only stretched and inflamed, so there was quite a lot Russell could do.

He massaged the joint carefully and showed her some gentle exercises to get it moving. Every couple of days, he used special machines to help her heal: one that calmed the inflammation by passing ultrasound waves through it and another one that used electric currents in the same way. The second one tingled a lot, but at least Lucy felt it was working!

Slowly, she regained her fitness. She started back to class with very basic exercises and tried to do a bit more each day, making sure to stop if her ankle hurt or felt tired. Then, when Russell agreed, she went through her clown routine very slowly and carefully.

"Is there any pain at all?" asked Mrs. Matthews, watching Lucy dance.

"No, there really isn't," Lucy answered with feeling. She knew how tempted she would be to say this even if it weren't true, but she also knew how silly that would be. Anyway, she didn't have to tell a lie because her ankle really didn't hurt anymore!

Just to be sure, she had to run through her dance again the next day, but once it was clear that everything was okay, Lucy was able to start rehearsing with the company again. She'd had a close call. Opening night was only two weeks away.

Those weeks passed by in a flash, and suddenly, it was opening night. All day, the students found it hard to concentrate in ballet class, and almost impossible in science and math. Then, late in the afternoon, they all piled on the school bus and set out for the Opera House. First, they had a light meal in the cafeteria, and then they did a warm-up session in one of the rehearsal studios before they were taken to their dressing rooms—one for the boys and one for the girls. Both rooms were equipped with long counters below tall, brightly lit mirrors and, underneath, a row of chairs that marked each performer's place.

Dressers bustled around, making sure each costume had all its pieces and was hung near the person who would be wearing it. Meanwhile, makeup and hair people offered whatever help was needed. Since mice didn't wear makeup, Lucy could sit quietly and watch, and she was fascinated to see Sarah and Joy transformed with rosy cheeks, long eyelashes, and thick, glossy ringlets for the party scene.

Suddenly, the stage manager's voice came over the loudspeaker, "Ladies and gentlemen, this is your half-hour call. Half an hour, ladies and gentlemen, half an hour."

This gave everyone plenty of warning, so that when the final call came, "Beginners! Beginners to the stage now please," they were all ready. The party guests headed for the door. Lucy and the other mice still had a little time though, since they weren't in the first scene.

THE NUTCRACKER

Ballet in   **Two Acts**

Music by Pyotr Ilyrich Tchaikovsky
Artistic Director Jeremy Wyatt
Conducted by Johann Cantoni
Choreography by Lev Ivanov
Set design by Justin Matthews
Costume design by Elaine Berlaise

The Nutcracker Prince	Juan Rivera
Sugar Plum Fairy	Fiona Peters
Clara	Sarah Chan
Mouse King	Dmitri Berlanga
Mother Gigogne	Crystal Lapetra

COMPOSER

Pyotr Ilyich Tchaikovsky
Birthplace Kamski-Votkinsk, Russia (1840–1893)
Training Trained as a lawyer in St. Petersburg
Affiliations Resigned his government position in 1862, Moscow Conservatoire teacher, composer, and conductor (Russia, Europe, US)
Other work Operas including *Eugene Onegin*, *The Queen of Spades*; Ballets including *Swan Lake, Sleeping Beauty, The Nutcracker*
Other information Recipient of Order of Vladimir (1884), Nominated Member of the Académie Française (1892), Honorary Doctorate in Music from Cambridge University, UK

PRINCIPALS

Juan Rivera
Birthplace Rio de Janeiro, Brazil
Training Centro de Dança Rio,
Royal Ballet Upper School
Previous company Ballet Nacionel
de Santiago de Chile
Favorite roles Albrecht in *Giselle*,
Solor in *La Bayadère*, Des Grieux in *Manon*

Sarah Chan
Birthplace Kushiro, Japan
Training Kushiro Ballet Academy,
English National Ballet School
Previous company Hong Kong Ballet
Favorite roles The Chosen One
in *The Rite of Spring*, Odette/Odile,
Sylph in *La Sylphide*

Fiona Peters
Birthplace London, UK
Training Arts Educational School
London, Royal Ballet Upper School
Favorite roles Swanilda
in *Coppélia*, Giselle, Juliet,
Odette/Odile in *Swan Lake*

Dmitri Berlanga
Birthplace St. Petersberg, Russia
Training Vaganova Ballet Academy
Previous company Maryinsky Ballet
Favorite roles The Russian Dance in
The Nutcracker, Tybalt in *Romeo and
Juliet*, Albrecht in *Giselle*

Crystal Lapetra
Birthplace Barcelona, Spain
Training Pastora Martos School, Paris Opera Ballet School
Previous company Vienna Staatsoper Ballet
Favorite roles Sugar Plum Fairy in *The Nutcracker*,
Gerda in *The Snow Queen*, Carmen in *Carmen*

ARTISTS OF THE COMPANY (CORPS OF BALLET)
Sayako Ang, Francis Bosch, Grant Freeman, Daniel Johnson,
Anton Kremen, Keon Luko, Ruth Parker, Michelle Percy,
Amber Ransell, Kaine Rich, Tamsin Scott, Laurretta Sousa,
Shua Tao, Adela Ward, Mark Wicks

STUDENTS FROM THE ACADEMY
Lucy Carr, Sarah Collings, Laurence Friesen, Jordan Garn,
Emilie Grute, Joy Kennedy, Connor Morley, Joseph Trendel

Everyone felt nervous standing in the wings, but once the mice went on stage, Lucy and the other young dancers lost themselves in the magic of the performance. Even though they knew the music so well, the live orchestra made it sound completely, overwhelmingly different.

Through tiny eyeholes in her headdress, Lucy looked out over the auditorium—a ring of soft lights around the edge glowed just bright enough so she could make out the shape of hundreds of people in the audience, all watching her and the other mice. The impression was spellbinding, and Lucy was very glad her position was at the back, hidden in the shadows, so she could take it all in before she and the rest of the mice pranced forward for the attack.

They lost their battle, as *Nutcracker* mice always do, and before the interval, they were back in the dressing room with the party guests, who had finished first. Most of them were chattering happily, delighted they had gotten through their dance without any disasters. For Lucy, Sarah, and a few others, however, the big moment was yet to come in Act II.

There was lots of fuss around them with makeup and wigs and costumes, but they were very glad they weren't being left to wait and worry on their own. When their call came, they made their way to the backstage area. Lucy considered it a very good omen that Fiona Peters, decked out as the Sugar Plum Fairy, was standing in the wings a few feet away with her personal dresser. Lucy had no time to gaze though, since she had to get ready for her entrance.

In the ballet, when Clara and the Nutcracker Prince arrive in the Land of Sweets, the Sugar Plum Fairy arranges a selection of dances for them and at the end of these a huge, jolly figure named Mother Gigogne arrives on stage wearing an enormous skirt. The dancer playing this character enters on stilts hidden underneath the skirt. Now, Lucy and the other clowns were concealed underneath the skirt, too, and they made their stage entrance shuffling along in the dark.

All her life Lucy would remember the moment when the skirt fabric parted like curtains and they all tumbled out and began their mischievous, bouncing dance. She was actually performing on the stage in the spotlight! Lucy knew she was dancing well. She delighted in every step and she felt as if she were in another world. It was a feeling she would spend the rest of her life longing to recapture.

Then the music stopped, and Lucy and the other clowns ran off. At first, all she could do was bend over, shut her eyes, and try to catch her breath. She was aware of a slight commotion nearby though and quickly recognized the voice of Fiona Peters.

"It can't have gone far… I had it a moment ago… does anybody have a flashlight?"

The dresser was trying to calm the fretful ballerina, but this was a major disaster. Fiona Peters had dropped the lucky penny she had rubbed before every stage entrance she had made since she was in the corps de ballet. And in a few moments, she was going on for the big pas de deux with the Nutcracker Prince.

Lucy still hadn't recovered from her very energetic dance, but all around her she was aware of people searching the floor. Then when she opened her eyes, the first thing she saw was a tiny glint underneath a piece of scenery nearby. Lucy reached down, ran her fingers over the grubby boards and felt something small, hard, and cool in her fingers—a penny!

Without stopping to think, she rushed over to the anxious Sugar Plum Fairy and held up her find. "Is this it?" she asked shyly.

The answer didn't come in the form of words, but as a huge, grateful bear hug.

"Oh, you darling girl, thank you, thank you!" The next moment, the gallant Nutcracker Prince led his partner onto the stage.

The Nutcracker Review

On New Year's Eve, I went to see *The Nutcracker*. This wonderful ballet opens with a Christmas party and is perfect as a festive treat. The heroine is Clara, who is given a nutcracker doll at the party. In the middle of the night, the doll turns into a handsome prince, who takes her on an enchanted journey.

My most memorable part of the ballet was when Clara crept downstairs on Christmas Eve to play with her doll. The tree suddenly started to grow and other strange things began to happen.

I adored the shimmering snowflakes. These appeared in the Land of Snow, the first stop on Clara's journey. The dancers were delicate, silvery flakes, fluttering and swirling.

I loved the exotic dances in the Kingdom of Sweets. There were bouncing Chinese characters, slinky Arabian dancers, a dramatic Russian troupe, and shepherdesses accompanied by musicians playing reed flutes.

My favorite dance was at the end of Clara's journey. The Prince and the Sugar Plum Fairy, who rule over the Kingdom of Sweets, perform a beautiful pas de deux for her. It was fairy magic!

Other Dances, Other Lands

Many ballets honor traditional folk dances by including them in the plot. These national dances provide a change of pace from classical movements and sometimes offer young artists, who are in the corps de ballet, a chance to perform in a small group.

Pole position

Across Europe, dances around the maypole are an ancient spring tradition. In *La Fille Mal Gardée*, village girls perform a ribbon dance. Each girl holds the end of a colored ribbon anchored to the pole. As they weave around each other, the ribbons are braided on the pole. To unravel them, the dancers reverse their steps.

Stamping and twirling

Folk dances appeared in ballet for the first time in an 1870 version of *Coppélia*, during the town celebrations. In this ballet, there is both a Hungarian czardas [*CHAR-dash*], shown above, and a Polish mazurka. Originally performed only by men, the czardas starts slowly and builds to a fast, rousing finish.

Leaping warriors

In *The Nutcracker*, when Clara and her Prince arrive in the Kingdom of Sweets, he arranges a celebration of dances from around the world. One of the best loved is the Russian dance, inspired by the traditional trepak performed by Cossack warriors. The music is based on traditional folk tunes.

RUSSIA

HUNGARY

ITALY

Party entertainment

The Queen arranges a grand ball in *Swan Lake*. During the evening, the guests are entertained by a display of national dances: a czardas, a mazurka, a Spanish dance, and a Neapolitan dance from Italy (shown).

Chapter 7
On Her Way...

The new semester had just begun, and Lucy could hardly believe she was in her final year at the Academy. She had passed so many milestones on her way: deciding to study ballet seriously, getting through all her dance exams, succeeding at both her auditions for the school, and building each year on what she learned and on the strengths and skills she gained.

When Lucy looked back on her time at the Academy, the single moment that meant the most to her was performing on stage in that first *Nutcracker*. After that, all her ambitions were even clearer and stronger and brighter. However, there was so much for Lucy to continue to think about and work on…

In this final year, the boys and girls came together for partnering classes for the first time. After years of learning how to place her body, how to balance, turn, jump, and coordinate, Lucy had to begin working with a partner guiding her, supporting her, and moving with her.

The first class was the hardest. The students were paired off according to height and, to a certain extent, personality. Lucy found herself working with a boy she didn't know very well, but had seen around school. Looking a little shy, he put out his hand and said, "Hi, I'm Mark."

"Hi, I'm Lucy," she answered, and feeling every bit as awkward, offered her hand back. They both realized though that they would have to get past this shyness to move on, and within a very short time, they did just that.

Soon, Lucy was looking forward to the classes. She worked with Mark quite a lot, first on simple balances and later on more complex movements and positions. However, it was important for her to gain experience with other boys, too, and she quickly stopped feeling self-conscious with every new partner so she could concentrate on these new skills.

For the rest of the year, the final-year students worked together on a simplified form of pas de deux known as "supported adage." It would be some time until they attempted more dramatic lifts and holds.

Lucy was hugely impressed by how strong the boys were, and how hard they worked to gain that strength—in addition to attending dance classes, they also trained constantly with body-building equipment and weights to prepare their bodies, especially their upper bodies, for partnering. She found it astonishing to realize that male dancers are just as fit and powerful as Olympic athletes, yet they have to remember steps and move gracefully, too!

Once Christmas passed, Lucy and her fellow students couldn't help being obsessed about moving up to the Senior School, which was linked with the ballet company. From here, the best dancers would be offered places in this company or another one, maybe in a different city or even a different country. The final-year students were not allowed to apply though. Instead, only a select group of the most promising students would be invited to audition.

On a particular day, all the students were to be interviewed separately and told whether they had been chosen.

The morning of the interviews arrived. Lucy ran into Sarah between classes. Lucy didn't have her interview until the afternoon, so she was still nervous.

"It's okay, I've been asked to audition," confided Sarah. Lucy was delighted to hear it.

Later, between classes, Jessie nearly knocked Lucy down. "I'm in! I'm in!" she shouted, but after that, Jessie couldn't really say anything sensible. She just kept letting out little squeals and grinning.

Lucy's interview with Mrs. Matthews was at three thirty. She didn't think it was possible to feel as tense as this without exploding. Once she was in the office, she didn't have to wait long.

"Congratulations!" said Mrs. Matthews, giving Lucy an affectionate hug. "Lucy, we would very much like you to audition for the Senior School, and we wish you the best of luck."

From their dormitory, only Joy was left out of the auditions, but her reaction was sensible. "Ballet is a very hard world, and I know in my heart it's not for me. I love dancing and I'll still do as much as I can, but I just don't want to worry about it all the time!"

Lucy, Sarah, Jessie, and the others had their audition at the Senior School itself. The building was in the middle of the city. Instead of being old and beautiful inside, the school felt bright and modern, which the students found exciting.

The audition class was far more advanced than the one they had done all those years ago, and it was scary in different ways. So much would depend on the decision made. Joining the Senior School was one step nearer to joining the company, and the dancers who didn't get in would have to find a new place to study and a new career path.

This time though, at least, the candidates all knew each other and the teachers. They were also older, so they didn't feel quite so overwhelmed.

How did this audition class differ from the previous one for the Junior School years ago?

As before, Lucy enjoyed the audition, losing herself in the music and the movement. When she left the building, she stopped at the door, turned to take a last look, and made a silent vow to return.

Luckily, the candidates only had to wait a few days, and they were given their results face-to-face. As Lucy made her way to Mrs. Matthews' office, images passed through her mind of all the other times she had made that journey. As always, she tapped on the door and went in. Instantly, she had a crystal-clear picture of the day the letter arrived with the news that she had passed her first Academy audition. This time though, it wasn't her mother in front of her, but otherwise, the scene was exactly the same—the smiling face of someone she trusted revealed her future without a single word being spoken.

Dances for Two

Girls and boys work together on pas de deux [*pah-de-DUH*], which is translated from French to mean "step for two." However, this ballet term can have a much more precise meaning, too.

The classical way

In classical (usually 19th-century) ballets, pas de deux have a formal structure. They begin with an adagio (slowish section), followed by a solo for him (male variation), and one for her (female variation), then another one for him and for her. At the end there is a fast section that they dance together called the coda.

In the famous "Black Swan" pas de deux from *Swan Lake*, the magician's daughter pretends to be the Swan Queen. She dances with the Prince and fools him.

118

Modern moves

Twentieth-century ballets are less formal in structure and in style, so the pas de deux have no strict divisions. They just flow from movement to movement, and the speed varies with the mood of the scene.

In *Romeo and Juliet*, Romeo falls in love with Juliet at her parents' ball. Later that night, when she is on her balcony, he calls to her and she runs to meet him.

Spartacus

Many people think of ballet as being mostly about girls in roles such as fairies, princesses, and swan maidens. However, one ballet, the Russian work *Spartacus*, created in 1968, has very few parts for women. All the leading characters and the entire corps de ballet are men.

◁ Act I

The Roman general Crassus returns to Rome in a triumphal procession. Among his prisoners are Spartacus and his wife, Phrygia. Their captors separate them.

As entertainment for drunken party guests Spartacus is forced to fight as a gladiator. After he kills a fellow slave, his despair and guilt inspire him to lead the slaves in a rebellion.

△ Act II

Spartacus and the rebels break into Crassus's villa and disrupt a lavish party. Spartacus challenges Crassus to a hand-to-hand fight and wins. He refuses to kill Crassus, however, and leaves him shamed and dishonored instead.

▷ Act III

Crassus gathers a large army to attack the rebels' camp. Spartacus decides to go into battle, but some of the rebels desert him. Eventually, the weakened forces are surrounded by Roman troops and Crassus, seeking revenge, makes sure the fight ends in Spartacus's death.

BALLET ACADEMY QUIZ

See if you can remember the answers to these questions about what you have read.

1. What is the ballet term for a bounce or spring?
2. In which Russian city is the Imperial Ballet Company?
3. Who was the first ballerina to wear pointe shoes?
4. What was Anna Pavlova's most famous role?
5. Which ballet did Lucy appear in and what were her roles?
6. What are modern tutus called?
7. Which animal's head does the fairy Puck give Bottom in *The Dream*?

8. What is the name of the old toymaker in *Coppélia*?
9. Which student was an understudy in *The Nutcracker*?
10. Who is Rothbart in *Swan Lake*?
11. What French term means a dance for two people?
12. From which country does the czardas originate?
13. Describe the colorful pattern on Lucy's clown costume.
14. What are the wilis in *Giselle*?
15. When was the first national ballet school founded and in which country?

Answers on page 125.

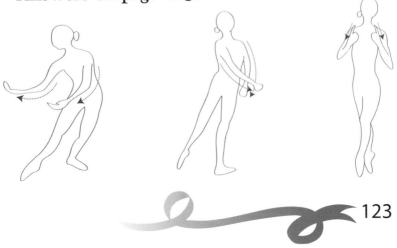

Glossary

Academy
A school or college that provides training in a specialized subject, especially in the arts and the sciences.

Assessment
A test to check someone's physical condition, ability, or knowledge.

Audition
An interview for a singing, acting, or dancing position where a candidate demonstrates his or her skills.

Auditorium
The area of a theater or concert hall where the audience sits.

Barre
A bar positioned at waist level for a dancer, as a support while doing exercises.

Choreographer
Someone who arranges and directs ballets and other forms of dance.

Corps de ballet
The dancers in a ballet company who perform in a group and not as soloists.

Dormitory
A large bedroom for a number of people to share.

Instep
The arched part between the ball of the foot and the ankle.

Interval
A period of time that provides a break in a performance.

Nutritionist
Someone who gives advice on healthy eating habits.

Physiotherapist
Someone who helps injured or disabled people through movement and exercise.

Prima ballerina
The title given to the main female dancer in a ballet company.

Technician
Someone whose job is to use and look after machines, electronic and other scientific equipment.

Technique
The way a task or movement is carried out.

Answers to the Ballet Academy Quiz:
1. Ballon; **2.** St. Petersburg; **3.** Marie Taglioni; **4.** The Dying Swan; **5.** *The Nutcracker*, a mouse and a clown; **6.** French or pancake tutus; **7.** A donkey; **8.** Dr. Coppélius; **9.** Jessie; **10.** An evil magician; **11.** Pas de deux; **12.** Hungary; **13.** Bright yellow with pink dots; **14.** Ghosts of young girls; **15.** 1713, France.

Index

About the Author

Lorrie Mack is a writer and editor specializing in various aspects of design and the arts. She is the author of a number of DK adults' and children's books, including *The Book of Dance*, and she has written and contributed to books about art, animals, and landscapes. At one time, Lorrie studied ballet extensively, and she continues to enjoy dancing in many different forms, including jazz, salsa, line-dancing, and court dances of the Renaissance movement.

About the Consultant

Dr. Linda Gambrell, Distinguished Professor of Education at Clemson University, has served as President of the National Reading Conference, the College Reading Association, and the International Reading Association. She is also reading consultant to the *DK Readers*.

Here are some other
DK Adventures you might enjoy.

Terrors of the Deep
Marine biologists Dom and Jake take their deep-sea submersible down into the world's deepest, darkest ocean trench, the Mariana Trench.

Horse Club
Emma is so excited—she is going to horseback-riding camp with her older sister!

In the Shadow of the Volcano
Volcanologist Rosa Carelli and her son, Carlo, are caught up in the dramatic events unfolding as Mount Vesuvius reawakens.

The Mummy's Curse
Are our intrepid time travelers cursed? Experience ancient Egyptian life along the banks of the Nile with them.

Clash of the Gladiators
Travel back in time to ancient Rome, when gladiators entertained the crowds. Will they be spared death?

Galactic Mission
Year 2098: planet Earth is dying. Five schoolchildren embark on a life or death mission to the distant star system of Alpha Centauri to find a new home.

Twister: A Terrifying Tale of Superstorms
Jeremy joins his cousins in Tornado Alley for vacation. To his surprise, he discovers they are storm chasers and has the ride of his life!